Wonders of Nature
Rainbows

Dana Meachen Rau

Marshall Cavendish
Benchmark
New York

You can make a rainbow. On the next sunny day, spray the garden hose. You will see a rainbow in the water.

You might see a rainbow in the spray from a fast boat. You might see a rainbow in a fountain.

You might see a rainbow in a waterfall.

A rainbow needs light and water to form. We see rainbows when sun and rain are in the sky at the same time.

The sun shines through the
raindrops to make the rainbow.

The best time to see a rainbow is late in the day in summer. Near the end of a *rainstorm*, the sun may start to come out. Stand outside so that the sun is behind you and the rain is in front of you. You might be able to spot a rainbow in the sky.

The rainbow got its name because it is shaped like the *bow* of a bow and arrow.

Long ago, some people
thought it was a bridge or path
from the earth to the sky.

A rainbow looks curved to people on the ground. That is because a rainbow is part of a circle.

If you were in an airplane, the rainbow might be a full circle. You would be at the point in the middle.

Light is always traveling from the sun to the earth. Light does not seem to have a color. But light is really made up of lots of colors.

15

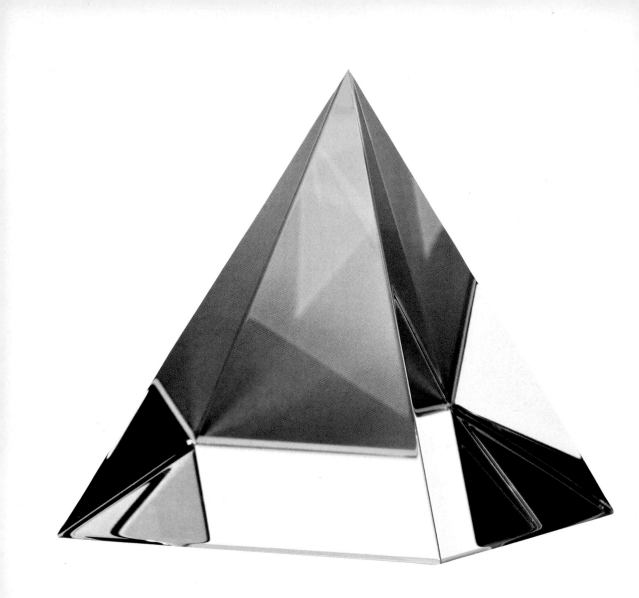

16

You can see all of light's colors with a *prism*. A prism is a clear block with three sides. Prisms are made of plastic or glass.

Sunlight goes through a prism. The prism bends the light. It breaks the light into all of its colors.

The colors in sunlight are red, orange, yellow, green, blue, *indigo*, and violet.

A raindrop bends light like a prism. The sunlight goes into the round raindrop. Then it bounces off the back of the raindrop. It comes out *divided* into all of its colors.

23

The colors in a rainbow are always the same. Red is always on the top curve of the rainbow. Violet is always on the bottom.

Sunlight shines through the
millions of raindrops in the sky.
Each drop breaks the light
into the rainbow colors.

Millions of drops together make
the rainbow you can see.

When the rain ends,
the rainbow starts to *fade*
away. Then you have a
clear, sunny sky.

Challenge Words

bow (BOH)—A tool made of curved wood and string that shoots arrows.

divided (di-VIED-ed)—Broken or cut into parts.

fade (FADE)—To disappear slowly.

indigo (IN-di-goh)—A color that is a mix of blue and violet.

prism (PRIZ-uhm)—A glass or plastic block with triangle-shaped ends that breaks up light.

rainstorm (RAIN-storm)—A storm with dark clouds and lots of rain.

Index

Page numbers in **boldface** are illustrations.

With thanks to Nanci Vargus, Ed.D.,
and Beth Walker Gambro, reading consultants

Marshall Cavendish Benchmark
99 White Plains Road
Tarrytown, New York 10591-9001
www.marshallcavendish.us

Library of Congress Cataloging-in-Publication Data

Rau, Dana Meachen, 1971–
Rainbows / by Dana Meachen Rau.
p. cm. — (Bookworms. Wonders of nature)
Summary: "Provides a basic introduction to rainbows,
including how and when they are formed"—Provided by publisher.
Includes index.
ISBN 978-0-7614-2669-1
1. Rainbow—Juvenile literature. I. Title. II. Series.
QC976.R2R38 2007
551.56'7—dc22
2006038622

Editor: Christina Gardeski
Publisher: Michelle Bisson
Designer: Virginia Pope
Art Director: Anahid Hamparian

Photo Research by Anne Burns Images

Cover Photo by *Corbis*/Royalty Free

The photographs in this book are used with permission and through the courtesy of:
Photo Researchers: pp. 1, 24 Michael P. Gadomski; p. 7 Michael Lustbader; p. 10 Leonard Lee Rue III;
p. 11 P. Jude; p. 19 Lawrence Lawry; p. 27 Gregory Ochocki; p. 29 Kevin Schafer.
SuperStock: p. 2; p. 5 Tom Murphy; p. 6 Ingram Publishing; pp. 8, 12, 26 age fotostock;
pp. 15, 23 Koji Kitagawa; p. 16 Brand X. *Corbis*: p. 4 Michele Chaplow; p. 13 Galen Rowell.
Index Stock Imagery: p. 20.

Printed in Malaysia
1 3 5 6 4 2